Victoria & Albert

A Royal Love Story

BRENDA WILLIAMS

'There was once a princess who lived with her mother in a palace. She had no father, no friends of the same age, and was hardly ever allowed to be by herself. Her companions were her widowed mother, an older half-sister, her governess, her dolls and her pets. At the age of 11, the princess learned that one day she was almost certain to be Queen, and she promised solemnly to be good. And so it was; she did become Queen, when she was just 18. Soon she had fallen in love with a handsome prince from across the sea. Being queen, she proposed, not he. The young prince was sad to leave his homeland, knowing he could never again be master of his own fate. Yet he did his best to adapt to his new life. The young queen and her charming prince married and lived very happily. They raised a large family, and their loving partnership became an example to all. When the prince died, still in the prime of life, the Queen was heartbroken. For the rest of her life, she treasured the memories of their time together, and when she was very old, and famous throughout the world, the prince remained the person closest to her heart.'

So might the romance of Victoria and Albert have been told as a nursery tale. Yet this love story was set in the real world, with an impact on history. It marked a turning point for Britain's royal family, and to the queen in particular love and marriage proved a source of strength and comfort. The two young people were brought together, like so many royal couples, by the scheming of matchmakers. The aftermath was not always easy. Albert's adopted country remained wary of his intelligence and seriousness, most people as unaware of his private playfulness as they were of the contrasting aspects of Victoria's own character.

Victoria & Albert: A Royal Love Story tells of a young couple's love: how the two grew up, what they were like, how they first met. Love deepened within their marriage, as they became partners in private and in public, at home with their family and ever on duty as sovereign and consort.

RIGHT: While fulfilling their duty in partnership, Victoria and her handsome prince enjoyed lighter moments, as shown in this sheet music illustration to *The Queen & Prince Albert's Polka*.

Introduction

Growing Up

ABOVE: Princess
Victoria with
her mother the
Duchess of Kent,
in mourning dress.
Painted in 1821 by
William Beechey,
the child clutches
a portrait of her
dead father.

Victoria, daughter of the Duke and Duchess of Kent, was born at
Kensington Palace on 24 May 1819: 'a pretty little Princess, as
plump as a partridge' in the eyes of her relieved and delighted
parents. Her mother Victoire was a German princess, whose
first husband had died in 1814. Still in her thirties, and with two healthy
children, in 1818 she had married the Duke of Kent, fourth son of King
George III. The Duke, a possible future king himself, had moved his
household from Germany during the last weeks of his wife's pregnancy, to
ensure the baby would be born on British soil. He was besotted with his
new daughter.

LEARNING THE TRICKS

If fussed over by her elderly 'Uncle King' (George IV), Victoria knew how to respond: asked at Windsor to choose a piece of music, she suggested 'God Save the King'.

Albert's Troubled Family

The Duchess soon received news of another happy event. Her brother Ernest, Duke of Saxe-Coburg-Saalfeld, had a second son, born on 26 August 1819. The birth was attended by the same midwife, Frau Siebold, who had brought Victoria into the world. The boy was named Francis Albert Augustus Charles Emmanuel.

Albert was a pretty child, with blue eyes and curly hair, like his mother. His older brother Ernest resembled their father. Duke Ernest had married in 1817, taking for his bride Princess Louise of Saxe-Coburg-Altenburg. At 16 she was half his age, intelligent and attractive, but the marriage was unhappy. Duke Ernest was a philanderer, Louise fell for another man, and in 1824 she was expelled from Coburg. Albert never saw his mother again. After his parents divorced in 1826, Louise married again, but died in Switzerland in 1831. When Saalfeld was exchanged for Gotha in 1825, Ernest became Duke of Saxe-Coburg-Gotha, the title Albert's brother later inherited.

ABOVE: Nine-year-old Prince Albert, blue-eyed and fair-haired. An intelligent and sensitive boy, this likeness is from a portrait by Schneider after Eckhardt, c. 1828.

Victoria's Childhood

Victoria's father enjoyed late parenthood all too briefly. On 23 January 1820, the Duke of Kent died, after taking ill while the family wintered in Devon. On George III's death six days later, his son the Prince Regent became King George IV - and Princess Victoria moved up the ladder of royal succession. The girl impressed visitors as lively and vigorous, with a growing sense of her own position. She grew up at Kensington Palace with her mother, her half-sister Feodore, nurse Mrs Brock ('Boppy'), governess Louise Lehzen, and her father's former equerry, Captain John Conroy. Conroy managed the household. With six children of his own to support, Kensington Palace offered him better prospects than a return to the army.

Mother and daughters slept in the same room, and the little princess saw few children of her own age, other than the Conroys. Tutored in a regulated routine of lessons and play, she gave her affection to pets, and dolls (she had well over a hundred), finding emotional release in drawing, and later in keeping a diary.

'I will be good'

Victoria's half-sister Feodore was 12 years older, intelligent and kind-hearted. She proved a loving companion, sharing Victoria's bedroom and her confidences. It was distressing when in 1828 Feodore left home to marry Prince Ernst of Hohenlohe-Langenburg. Letters kept the sisters in contact, and Feodore later told Victoria that she was glad to escape 'that miserable existence' within Kensington Palace. However, it was not all misery. And in 1830, Victoria's future regal status came closer.

On 26 June 1830, George IV died at 62. Victoria, now 11, became next in line to the throne after her uncle, the new King William IV. Since Uncle Billy had no legitimate heirs, it was almost certain that one day she would be Queen. This realisation spurred her famous vow, 'I will be good'.

ABOVE: The Prince Regent, later George IV, painted by Sir Thomas Lawrence around 1814.

Leopold's Dreams

Others were also aware of Victoria's changing status. Her German uncle Leopold had given shrewd advice to the Duchess of Kent, his sister, and now took more than a passing interest in his niece. Leopold had almost become a royal British consort himself, by marrying Princess Charlotte, daughter of George IV. He had lost Charlotte in childbirth in 1817, but his hopes and family ambitions remained. In 1830, Leopold was chosen as the first king of newly-created Belgium. New responsibilities did not divert him from intrigues in Britain – or Coburg, where he had two nephews: Ernest and Albert. One or other might bid for the hand of his niece Victoria. They were cousins, so it was natural they might meet.

ABOVE: William IV in court dress with Queen Adelaide. The engraving of 1832 shows Victoria's kindly aunt bedecked in flounces and feathers.

The King and Conroy

William IV, the 'sailor king', was impressed by Victoria's strong character, and his wife Queen Adelaide was genuinely fond of the child. Both were suspicious of the Kensington Palace household, hearing scandalous rumours of a relationship between Conroy and the Duchess. Such tales grew more alarming when the Duchess was named as future regent, to act for Victoria should the girl come to the throne before the age of 18. There were royal rows with Conroy – about flying the royal standard on a ship with Victoria aboard, and even over arrangements for Victoria's confirmation in 1835. Caught in the crossfire, and after an exhausting tour in part planned by Conroy further to annoy the king, the teenage princess became seriously ill with fever.

ROYAL PROGRESS

As a child Victoria enjoyed Christmas, and summer trips to Bath, Ramsgate, Tunbridge Wells and noble houses such as Blenheim Palace. A less scenic tour of the Black Country and Birmingham was taken to show her the new industrial Britain.

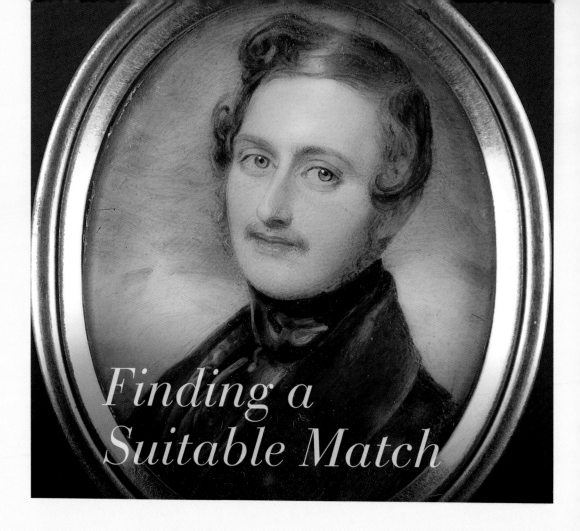

Finding a Suitable Match

When Victoria recovered, King William (himself in failing health) decided that his niece's future must be settled. He and Queen Adelaide had hopes of marrying Victoria to her cousin George, son of the Duke of Cambridge. The two were of the same age, though showed no deep affection. Victoria was fonder of her Cumberland cousin, also called George, but he had been blinded after an accident. Who else was eligible?

Marrying into the British aristocracy could create difficulties: family rivalries, jealousies, dangerous ambitions, political rifts. Foreigners were not often popular as consorts for British queens, but a friendly Protestant prince might be 'managed' by the Court and government. The king thought the solution might be found within the Dutch royal family.

The Coburg Connection

Victoria's uncle Leopold had his own candidate in mind. In Court circles the Coburgs were regarded as intriguers, but they had proved adept in marriage negotiations. Two of Albert's uncles and four aunts had all made good

LEFT: Prince Ernest, older brother of Albert, was raised with him almost as a twin and became Duke of Saxe-Coburg-Gotha in 1844. He and his wife, Princess Alexandrine of Baden, had no children.

marriages. Aunt Victoire had won the Duke of Kent; Uncle Leopold had married first Princess Charlotte, and then in 1832 Princess Louise-Marie, daughter of the king of France. Leopold's brother Ernest also married in 1832, his second wife being his sister's daughter, Marie of Württemberg. There were no children, but Marie grew fond of her two stepsons from the Duke's first marriage. Leopold could rely on her support, and on that of the boys' Coburg grandmother, the Dowager Duchess.

Which Brother?

Leopold had watched Albert grow up, under the influence of his teacher Albert Florschutz and Leopold's personal physician and adviser, Baron Christian Stockmar. Leopold preferred 16-year-old Albert to Ernest, 17, and Stockmar agreed, praising Albert's 'pleasant and striking features'. A diligent student, intelligent, serious-minded, but with a lighter side that enjoyed practical jokes and mimicry, the young man's present ambitions extended little further than university, and a quiet life in Coburg, which brother Ernest would one day rule. Albert must make a good marriage…

So why not pay a visit to cousin Victoria? The Duchess of Kent welcomed her brother's suggestion, and in May 1836, the Coburg boys set out for England.

LEFT: The Ehrenburg Palace in Bavaria, main residence of Coburg princes since the 1500s. Albert's birthplace was the Rosenau castle, deep in the nearby forest.

The Match Makers

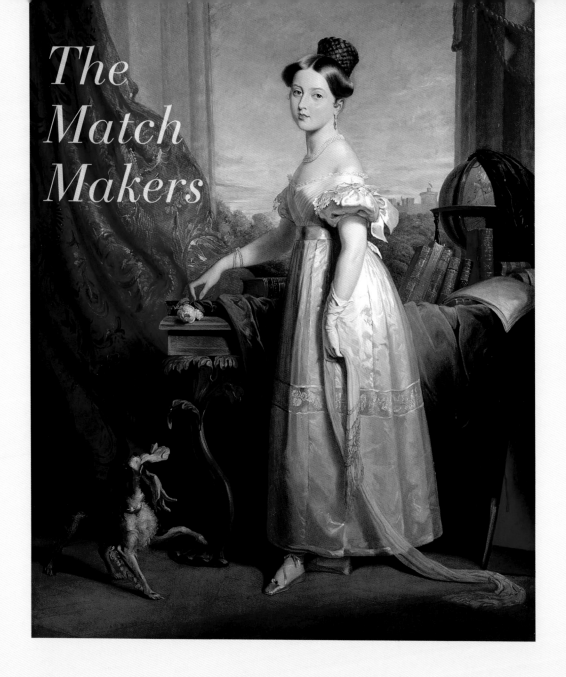

K ing William had already invited the Dutch Prince of Orange and his brother to come courting. He rebuffed the Coburg idea, yet Leopold would not be put off. He warned Victoria that the king might be rude to her German cousins, but stressed that they would be her guests and not the king's. With a cynical press noting that German princes were continuing 'to pour into this country' to woo the 'little Princess', Leopold complained that while relatives of the King and Queen 'to the God-knows-what degree' were made welcome, Victoria's own Coburg kin were kept away.

ABOVE: Princess Victoria at 16 with her spaniel Dash, painted by Sir George Hayter (1792–1871) around the time when Albert first saw her.

'Albert, who is just as tall as Ernest but stouter, is extremely handsome; his hair is about the same colour as mine; his eyes are large and blue, and he has a beautiful nose...'

FROM PRINCESS VICTORIA'S JOURNAL, WEDNESDAY 18 MAY 1836

Netherlands vs Coburg

The two Dutch princes were first seen by Victoria at a ball in St James's Palace. She was not smitten, writing to Uncle Leopold that Alexander seemed embarrassed. The young men were 'heavy, dull and frightened, and ... not at all prepossessing'. So much for the Oranges.

Within a week, on 18 May 1836, the Coburg contingent arrived. Victoria's sister Feodore had already given her opinion, in a letter sent in March. Albert was handsome, Ernest good-natured – and her favourite. Naturally, she was curious to learn what her younger sister thought. At first sight, according to her Journal, the princess found her German cousins 'most delightful', sensible and 'very fond of occupation' yet more worldly and fun than the stolid Oranges. An evening of opera confirmed a shared love of music, but they also liked animals, fresh air and exercise, which included dancing. The younger brother most pleased her, for Albert was 'extremely handsome'.

The cousins stayed for three weeks, a treat for Victoria, hitherto starved of company her own age. She might even believe herself in love, writing to Uncle Leopold with thanks for 'the prospect of great happiness...' in the person of 'dear Albert'. She knew full well what her uncle's hopes were.

RIGHT: The youthful Albert, in an engraving made three years before his marriage. Victoria noted in her diary his 'delicate moustachios' and 'slight whiskers'.

Treading Carefully

Leopold might congratulate himself that his niece was already half-won, and her mother gave Albert a ring with Victoria's name on it. When a new suitor was mooted, Prince Adalbert of Prussia, the Duchess of Kent dismissed him in a letter to his father. She was a Coburg, and the Coburgs were determined to back their runner. And Albert seemed to be favourite.

Albert Drags His Feet

Yet Albert seemed a reluctant starter. He complained to his stepmother Marie that the visit to Britain had made him unwell. The Channel crossing had been bad enough; then had come an exhausting royal round of concerts, birthday parties, dinners and a ball. Despite his manly appearance, Albert was more delicate than his brother. He needed early nights, having been

ABOVE: Leopold of Saxe-Coburg and Gotha, first king of the Belgians (1831), was instrumental in bringing about the marriage of his niece and nephew.

ABOVE: Stormy seas in the Channel made Albert's first visits to England unforgettable, and uncomfortable.

known to vanish during the day, to doze in an alcove. He had however been warmly received by his dear aunt Kent, and reported that 'our cousin [Victoria] is very amiable'.

These were hardly the words of a love-sick swain, yet Leopold was nothing if not optimistic.

Leopold's Waiting Game

Leopold had to tread carefully. His marriage to Princess Charlotte had won him the title of 'His Royal Highness', the Claremont estate in Surrey (a wedding gift from the nation), and an annuity. Even so, the new king of the Belgians was not altogether trusted in Britain, especially after marrying a French princess. His open advocacy of a Coburg marriage antagonised the king, and William had at one point wanted Ernest and Albert turned back at Dover. It took the diplomacy of Lord Melbourne, the prime minister, to dissuade him. Nevertheless, the king told Melbourne he would never consent to Victoria marrying a Coburg. Leopold would have to be patient; at least until the princess came of age on her 18th birthday – or the king died.

'He possesses every quality'

ictoria shed tears after her cousins departed, but she was made of stern stuff. Other duties awaited her. Besides, her memories, and her Journal, would sustain her. She had perhaps already concluded that, were she to marry, Albert was the preferred option.

Albert's Good Points

True, Albert had been unable to dance until 3 in the morning; rich food had caused him to have bilious attacks (noted in her Journal); and at late-night entertainments he had difficulty keeping awake. However, the last week had

ABOVE: Victoria as a young woman. This image from 1836 by French lithographer Emile Desmaisons portrays an ethereal princess. The real woman was more down to earth.

'Externally he has everything attractive to women, and possesses every quality they find pleasing at all times and in all countries.'

REPORT ON ALBERT FROM
STOCKMAR TO LEOPOLD

LEFT: William IV, painted in 1837, by Sir David Wilkie, Principal Painter in Ordinary to both William and Victoria. The king had decided ideas about suitable suitors for his niece.

been especially enjoyable, with piano duets, singing lessons, the opera, a service for poor children at St Paul's Cathedral, and a last happy breakfast on 10 June with her 'dear Uncle and those dearest, beloved Cousins…' And Albert had played so happily with her pet dog Dash.

Albert was full of 'goodness and sweetness', and impressed all with his cleverness. He was 'the most reflecting of the two' yet could also be so merry and gay and happy, 'as young people ought to be'. Just as important, he had won over King William, when they had met at a ball. Everyone had been astonished by the king's change of heart. Albert's stock rose.

Mind Made Up?

Victoria thanked Uncle Leopold for sending Albert to her. She was content, since 'he possesses every quality that could be desired to render me perfectly happy…'. Leopold was to take Albert under his special protection, and she hoped that 'all will go prosperously and well on this subject of so much importance to me'.

And then her mind returned to affairs at the Palace.

RIGHT: Woman at a window by Victoria, one of 119 sketches in a maroon leather folder inscribed with her name and dated 1836. Most of the drawings show figures and scenes from books or plays.

Queen at 18

Relations between the king and Victoria's mother were stormy. There was a tempest in August 1836, when the Duchess of Kent declined to attend the queen's birthday, and a positive hurricane when the king raged over her taking additional rooms in Kensington Palace without his consent. At his birthday dinner, William denounced 'evil advisers' at the duchess's side (meaning Conroy), and said she had insulted him by keeping Victoria away from Court. It was all very upsetting for a girl of 17, caught in the middle.

Family Tensions

The rest of 1836 passed quietly, with a holiday in Ramsgate, and a stay at Claremont, Leopold's estate, with time for the princess to practise her music and drawing. In the spring of 1837, however, came fresh disagreements between duchess and king, this time over royal protocol when the princess

ABOVE: Victoria's first Privy Council meeting, painted by Sir David Wilkie, 1838. The young queen meets her government ministers, and makes a good impression. Among those present were Lord Melbourne and the Duke of Wellington.

ABOVE: The Queen in regal splendour by Franz Winterhalter (1805–1873). The Imperial State Crown and state papers lie at her left hand, with Westminster beyond.

was on public view, and her income once she was of age. The king was keen to detach his niece from what he regarded as the pernicious environment of Kensington Palace.

Albert was out of sight, and almost out of mind. In 1837, he was sent away to university in Bonn. He was taken to Italy to study art and architecture, and by his father to Berlin for some racy nightlife. Albert chose books in preference.

Victoria's 18th birthday on 24 May 1837 was a turning point. Now, should Victoria become queen, her mother would no longer be required to act as regent. Leopold wrote commiserating on these 'battles and difficulties', urging his niece not to turn against her mother, but the tensions were never fully repaired.

Lord Melbourne

Melbourne was 56 when Victoria came to the throne. His wife, Lady Caroline Lamb, had died in 1828; their marriage had survived her scandalous affair with the poet Lord Byron. Their only son, who was disabled, died the year before Victoria became queen.

Becoming Queen

King William had been too ill to attend Victoria's birthday ball, and he died at Windsor during the night of 19/20 June 1837. The carriage bearing the message reached Kensington in the early hours, and the new queen was woken at 5, coming down in dressing-gown and slippers. Stockmar was at her side at breakfast. Victoria wrote letters to Leopold and Feodore, and sent a note to the bereaved Queen Adelaide. Just before nine, the prime minister Lord Melbourne saw her alone. And at 11.30 came her first Privy Council meeting. Life had changed for ever.

Marry for Love...

ABOVE: Victoria with
a rose, displaying
the Order of the
Garter on her
left arm. The
1842 painting
by Winterhalter
found a home at
Osborne House.

Melbourne now became the other key player in the love story, along with Leopold. Urbane and witty, the prime minister was rarely absent from the new queen's side. The nation's last queen regnant had been Anne, more than a century earlier. Everyone was learning to adapt to the new situation.

On 26 June 1837, Albert wrote from Germany offering congratulations on 'that great change which has taken place in your life'. Now that she was queen of 'the mightiest land in Europe', he trusted she would not forget her cousins in Bonn.

ABOVE: The royal bedroom at Buckingham Palace, by James Roberts, 1848. Here Victoria awoke on her coronation morning and wedding day, and gave birth to eight of her nine children.

A Room of One's Own

The queen had not forgotten, but had much to occupy her. Victoria moved out of her mother's room, and from July resided at Buckingham Palace. She enjoyed her new independence, even its responsibilities. She explored Windsor Castle, reviewed her soldiers on horseback, went to Brighton to see the Royal Pavilion, saw *Hamlet* and read Sir Walter Scott. Her demeanour through the ordeal of the coronation on 28 June 1838 impressed everyone.

The young queen spent hours talking, and listening, to Melbourne, this 'honest, clever and good man' who made her laugh, and yet knew so much about the world. He became an affectionate father-figure, free with his advice – such as walk more, and eat less, or become fat.

Victoria enjoyed her 20th birthday: 'out of my TEENS', she wrote joyfully, and celebrated by dancing her first mazurka at a ball with the Russian Grand Duke Alexander. Albert, far away and pursuing his studies, showed little sign of the impatient lover.

A Fretful Time

It was Leopold, in Belgium, who fretted. He saw Victoria in September 1838 but made little progress, so in June 1839 he suggested Albert make a second visit. The queen agreed, then changed her mind. She told Melbourne she might not marry since 'I shouldn't agree with anybody'. He mildly suggested she would be happier married, but she should marry only for love. Certainly, she must make a respectable marriage – no more scandals like those that had clung to her royal uncles, with their mistresses and illegitimate children.

There were other visitors to distract her: more young Coburg cousins – the children of Uncle Ferdinand ('dear, dear young people'), and a handsome soldier, Alexander Mensdorff-Pouilly (son of Aunt Sophia), who was terribly shy but had such attractive hair. And there were disagreeable political difficulties, especially the 'Bedchamber Crisis'. The marriage question seemed 'odious'. In July, she told Melbourne she preferred to wait a year or two, or not marry. 'I don't know about that,' the prime minister cautioned, though agreeing marriage was not to be rushed. The queen confided to her Journal that she had better wait 'till impatience was shown'. As yet, Albert was still showing no such signs.

The Bedchamber Crisis

With the Whig government tottering, Melbourne resigned in May 1839. The distressed queen asked the old Duke of Wellington, but he declined to become prime minister. Tory leader Sir Robert Peel was proposed, but (Victoria complained) 'behaved very ill' in seeking to replace her Ladies of the Bedchamber with ladies of his own political tinge. In the end, Peel gave up, and Melbourne was back at her side.

There is No Engagement...

I n July 1839, Victoria wrote to Leopold again. Was Albert aware of his family's hopes? There was 'no engagement between us', and in any case she would not make a 'final promise' for perhaps two to three years. The country was not ready for a foreign marriage. Besides, on seeing Albert again, she might well like him 'as a friend, and as a cousin, and as a brother, but not more'.

Gloomy Prospects?

This coyness worried Leopold, who also had concerns about Albert. The young man seemed reluctant to quit sleepy Coburg for turbulent Britain, to marry a young woman possibly as temperamental as her disreputable Hanoverian relations. Lurid stories reached Coburg. The young queen was frivolous, obsessed with Court ceremony, and (worse) liked to dance all night and sleep into the day. These were 'gloomy prospects', Albert told his tutor.

In August, Melbourne resumed his gentle prodding. Marry for love certainly, though a foreign prince would not be popular. The queen replied that she would do what was best for her country, but marrying a British subject would cause jealousies. Melbourne agreed. She said Albert was praised 'on all sides'. And he was very handsome.

Visits On and Off

Albert's return was proposed for 30 September, but then postponed by the queen. Such haste would make people think everything was settled. And she was very busy. It was then Albert's turn to delay. The visit slipped back, into October. Victoria now showed signs of irritation, even anxiety. Should not a lover be more eager? She wrote to Leopold on the first day of October, making the point.

When Albert and his brother finally left, they broke their journey to consult Uncle Leopold. Noting Albert's gloom, he despatched yet another letter: Victoria must try to cheer him up. In low spirits, and appalling weather, Albert set sail through rough seas for an uncertain future.

ALBERT'S RESOLVE

After his marriage, Albert wrote that he had set out on this journey resolved to wait no longer for Victoria to make up her mind. It is hard to tell if this later, considered view reflected his true state of mind in October 1839. On the awful sea crossing, he doubtless wished fervently to be back home.

OPPOSITE: Victoria's secret 24th birthday present for Prince Albert was this 1843 portrait by Winterhalter. In an intimate pose, with hair loose, it was intended for his eyes only. Her pendant holds a lock of his hair.

RIGHT: Albert in military dress, perhaps contemplating his marriage. Prints like this (about 1840, after Franz Hanfstaengl) were popular at a time when photography was still in its infancy.

'The happiest of human beings'

O
n Thursday 10 October 1839, after a storm-tossed Channel crossing by paddle steamer, the seasick-pale, exhausted Albert struggled up the great staircase of Windsor Castle at 7.30 pm. Victoria greeted him 'with some emotion'. The brothers' luggage had been left behind, so with no dress clothes they had to miss dinner. Supper in his room, and a wash and brush-up, so restored Albert that when the queen saw him after dinner, she was entranced.

It Must Be Love

Ernest had improved, she wrote to Leopold, but Albert's beauty was 'most striking', and he was 'excessively admired', for both looks and affability. Melbourne agreed, a fine young man. The next day, luggage having arrived, the three went horse-riding, and Victoria admired Eos, Albert's greyhound.

Love's dart had struck. The queen told Melbourne that her ideas on marriage were 'a good deal changed'. When Ernest became unwell, she had Albert to herself for riding, music and dancing. Within three days, she had told the prime minister she would marry him; his good temper would balance hers. Melbourne said he was glad, for she would be more

ABOVE: The Queen bejewelled with rubies, 1840, by John Partridge. Strikingly dressed, with lace trimmings, she wears a ferronière decoration across the forehead. Partridge was displaced as royal portraitist by the German Winterhalter.

'He seems perfection and I think that I have the prospect of very great happiness before me…'

VICTORIA IN A LETTER TO LEOPOLD
15 OCTOBER 1839

'Your prophecy is fulfilled… I will not let my courage fail…'

ALBERT IN A LETTER TO STOCKMAR
9 NOVEMBER 1839

'comfortable' with a husband. Now she must tell Albert. A brief engagement, secret at first: Parliament would have to approve Albert's title and allowance. A February wedding, he suggested.

The Proposal

Neither queen nor prime minister seems to have contemplated Albert's refusal. The proposal must come from her, as queen, so Victoria summoned Albert to a private meeting at lunchtime on 15 October 1839. She told him she would be 'too happy' if he would consent to her wish. He did consent; they embraced and kissed. The queen confided in her Journal that she felt 'the happiest of human beings'.

After lunch, Albert penned a love-note to his 'Dearest, greatly beloved Victoria'. He was fulsome: heaven had sent him an angel, he hoped he would make her as happy as she deserved, he was 'in body and soul ever your slave, your loyal Albert'. She too was busy with pen and ink, writing to Uncle Leopold. Albert's warm response had given her great pleasure; she would do her best to ease his sacrifice. She also wrote to Stockmar, telling him that 'Albert has completely won my heart'. Victoria's rapture was unconfined; Albert's more considered. The dream had become a reality. He wrote to tell his stepmother Marie how sad he would be to leave home; his future had 'certain dark sides'. However, as he told Stockmar, he would do his duty, and his best to win the respect, and love, of the queen and her country.

RIGHT: 'Albert will you marry me?' – a satirical print of 1840 entitled *Leap Year!* It shows one public view of the proposal, with Victoria persuading a coy Albert.

Albert's Arrival

ABOVE: Prince Albert carried to Dover in the steam packet *Ariel*. A flag-waving crowd, soaked to the skin, braves wind and waves to cheer him on. The picture by W. A. Knell, 1840, was bought by Albert the following year.

The young couple spent four weeks getting to know one another. Victoria waited until 10 November to tell her mother, and on the 14th Albert returned home, with a parting kiss. He had left a favourable impression. 'Well manner'd and handsome … said to be very well informed and sensible', commented Lady Cowper, Melbourne's sister.

Marrying for Money?

The royal love affair was not yet common knowledge, with no prying reporters nor intrusive cameras to pursue the couple. Melbourne worried about public reaction, but first there was official business. The Privy Council must be told, and the queen did so on 23 November, her hands shaking as she read the declaration of her forthcoming marriage. Parliament then debated Albert's future title, and income. Public reaction was slow and at first unenthusiastic. Few people had ever heard of Albert, or Coburg. And what about his religion? Were not many Germans Catholics? A popular view was that the queen had been snared by a hard-up European princeling after the country's money. Parliament voted Albert an allowance of £30,000 (Queen Anne's grant to her husband had been £50,000).

At home in Coburg, Albert took extra lessons to improve his English, and tried to understand the British constitution – or lack of one. He wrote to his fiancée, asking if he might have in his private household at least two or three

The Hopeful Suitor

'He comes to take for better or worse England's fat queen and England's fatter purse.'

LINES FROM A POPULAR SONG, REFERRING TO ALBERT

German friends. She told him no, he could rely on her to provide 'absolutely pleasant people'. His private secretary was already chosen, a Mr Anson. He must trust her to deal with politicians – only the Whigs (Melbourne and colleagues), not Peel's hateful Tories. Nerves increased royal tetchiness as the wedding day drew nearer.

The Groom Sets Forth

Albert's departure from Coburg saw the family entourage boosted with extra carriages sent by Victoria. The prince seemed resigned rather than eager. He rested in Belgium, where Leopold observed that the bridegroom seemed 'rather exasperated', even melancholy. After yet another stormy Channel crossing, the people of Dover turned out in the rain to cheer the unsteady groom. It was the same in Canterbury, and Londoners put out flags to welcome the Coburg carriages as on 8 February 1840 they clattered along the Mall. At the palace, the queen and her mother came out to welcome the travellers. Here at last, almost hers, was 'dearest, precious Albert'.

'I and Albert alone...'

There were the usual pre-wedding anxieties about guests, and bridesmaids, the bride's mother and the honeymoon. Albert asked for bridesmaids of the highest moral character. Lord Melbourne archly replied that among people of quality morality mattered less than rank, and rank would determine the train-bearers. Victoria agreed that her mother could ride with her in the carriage. Albert wanted an extended honeymoon at Windsor; Victoria said three days, for 'business can stop and wait for nothing'. Albert sighed. She gave in. They would have a week. The small Chapel Royal was chosen for the ceremony, rather than Westminster Abbey, in part to keep out unwelcome guests (such as Tory politicians). Clerks and clergy pored over dust-layered papers and books from Queen Anne's day to work out the appropriate service.

Victoria caught cold, and feared measles; Albert sent her some caricatures, which cheered her up. On the Sunday before the wedding, the couple exchanged gifts. Albert's included the star and badge of the Order of the Garter; he gave Victoria a sapphire brooch. They rehearsed the service, to be sure of their responses, including how to 'manage the ring'.

ABOVE: Victoria commissioned this painting from Winterhalter in 1847 as an anniversary gift for Albert. She is in her wedding dress of cream silk satin and Honiton lace. The queen was laid to rest with her wedding veil covering her face.

Wedding Day

Monday 10 February 1840 dawned wet and windy. The queen was regally hopeful – 'the rain will cease', she told Albert in a note written after breakfast. Had he slept well? She felt 'very comfortable'. Outside, crowds gathered, despite the weather, with many spectators standing on chairs, tables and barrels, and others perched in trees. Some branches broke, spilling their occupants onto those below.

Albert went to his wedding in the British army uniform of a field-marshal, under the stern gaze of the Tory Duke of Wellington, invited against the queen's wishes. The bride wore a white satin dress with Honiton lace, a diamond necklace and earrings, in a style much copied. (The wedding veil she later wore for her 1897 Jubilee photograph.) The queen processed up the aisle with twelve bridesmaids in her train, to the strains of the national anthem. She was given away by her uncle the Duke of Sussex, and she promised to 'obey'.

THE CONQUERING HERO

Albert entered the Chapel Royal to the music of 'See the Conquering Hero Comes'. For a young man of 20 never near a battle, this choice raised some eyebrows – including probably the Duke of Wellington's.

Tears of Delight

After the ceremony, the bride kissed Queen Adelaide – but only shook hands with her mother, weeping tears of relief and joy. Then came the wedding breakfast at Buckingham Palace, a banquet with a cake reputedly 9 feet round. Just before 4 pm, the couple drove off to Windsor, the bride in silk and swansdown, her bonnet trimmed with orange blossom. At last, as the queen wrote later, it was 'I and Albert alone, which was SO delightful.'

'Heavenly love...'

T he newly married couple ended the day at Windsor. Albert played the piano but Victoria was struck with a headache so severe she could not face dinner. She lay on a sofa, with Albert beside her on a stool. Even so, as she recorded in her Journal, the queen felt she had never known such 'heavenly love and happiness'. How thankful she was to have 'such a husband'.

Out and About

Next morning they were out and about early, enjoying one another's company and walking Albert's dog. Their first few weeks together unlocked reserves of passion in both, and confirmed shared loves of music, art, games, horse-riding and dancing. But there was always work. And from that Albert was, in most respects, at first excluded. Every day there were papers for the queen to read, letters to sign. He might sit beside her, but she was queen. Her energy lasted late into the night, at work or play; he was ready for bed by 10.

Both were still only 20. Albert knew that, whatever his own rank, he

ABOVE: Landseer's painting of the married couple at Windsor, begun in 1840. Albert the huntsman has his greyhound Eos at his feet. Eos ('very friendly if there is plum-cake in the room') was accidentally shot in 1842 by Victoria's uncle Ferdinand, but recovered and died in 1844 aged 11.

During her first pregnancy the queen began to share official work with Albert. She remembered the sad fate of Princess Charlotte (uncle Leopold's first wife). Childbirth was dangerous; Albert and the royal baby might be left to rule without her.

LEFT: An attempt on the queen's life. The contemporary lithograph shows Edward Oxford firing pistol shots at the royal carriage on Constitution Hill, 10 June 1840. Albert bravely shielded the pregnant Victoria. Oxford was found guilty but insane.

would never be the complete master in his own house. And naturalised though he was, he would never be an 'Englishman'. He was, however, very soon a father, and that changed things. The queen had hoped that pregnancy would not come too soon; but within two months it did. 'A sad business', she called it, in a letter to Leopold and complained to Albert's grandmother of being 'most unhappy'.

Family Life Begins

In June 1840, a disturbed teenager tried to shoot the queen as her carriage drove up Constitution Hill. Albert shielded her, the would-be assassin was arrested, and the prince's courage widely praised. More important, with the queen pregnant, her husband was made regent in the event of her death – a significant public promotion.

The queen hoped her baby would not be a 'nasty girl'. It was. The Princess Royal was born in November 1840. Quickly becoming pregnant again, however, Victoria in 1841 produced a son and heir, the Prince of Wales.

TOP: Victoria, the baby Princess Royal ('Pussy'), painted by Landseer in 1841 as a gift for Albert from his wife. Eos snuggles at her feet and a Barbary dove (perhaps symbolising innocence) perches on her chair. The picture hung in Albert's writing room at Buckingham Palace.

Loved and Lost

Victoria and Albert's love endured, and their marriage became the model of Victorian propriety. The royal couple made homes together, notably Balmoral in Scotland and Osborne on the Isle of Wight, for their family of nine children. They enjoyed Christmas and holidays, Scotland and the seaside. In 1842 they took their first train ride, and the following year visited France – the first visit by a reigning English monarch since Henry VIII. On the Isle of Wight, Albert made a beach hut, and Victoria tried bathing in the sea. For 21 years the couple were happy, and the country generally satisfied with this new-look 'royal family'.

Albert's Crowning Achievement

Albert's conscientious hard work culminated in the Great Exhibition of 1851, a celebration of artistic, industrial and scientific achievement that drew six million visitors to the Crystal Palace in Hyde Park. The couple's last child, Beatrice, was born in 1857, and Albert finally received the title of Prince Consort. In 1858, the Princess Royal, 'Vicky', was married. Everything seemed to be going well, apart from anxiety caused by the antics (real or rumoured) of the Prince of Wales, whom neither parent understood.

In November 1861, worn down by work and worry, Albert contracted typhoid. He sank rapidly, and with his wife and children at his bedside, died on 14 December. The queen was desolate. She wrote to Vicky, in Germany, wondering how she could live without 'those blessed arms' that had clasped her in 'the sacred hours at night'.

Younger daughter Alice, at 18, became her chief support, as Victoria retreated from public view for some years. She wore mourning black for the rest of her life. Albert's room was kept as he had left it, and the royal mausoleum at Frogmore became his memorial, along with others such as the Albert Memorial in London. Victoria found other rocks to rely on: her servants John Brown and Abdul Karim, and her favourite prime minister (after Melbourne), Benjamin Disraeli.

Victoria's love for Albert had restored public respect for the monarchy, and fruited across the royal families of Europe. As Queen-Empress and royal grandmother, she celebrated her Golden and Diamond Jubilees (1887, 1897), the most famous woman in the world. The end came with her death on 22 January 1901 at Osborne, the house which her beloved Albert had designed, his love sustaining her to the very end.

LEFT: A photograph by Roger Fenton, famed for his Crimean War studies. Having seen Fenton's work, Victoria commissioned portraits in 1854. Family and state responsibilities were taking their toll.

TO THE
QUEEN'S PRIVATE APARTMENTS

THE QUEEN AND PRINCE ALBERT AT HOME.